A Lamentation On Republican France

Edward St. John-Brenon

In the interest of creating a more extensive selection of rare historical book reprints, we have chosen to reproduce this title even though it may possibly have occasional imperfections such as missing and blurred pages, missing text, poor pictures, markings, dark backgrounds and other reproduction issues beyond our control. Because this work is culturally important, we have made it available as a part of our commitment to protecting, preserving and promoting the world's literature. Thank you for your understanding.

DEDICATED TO NAPOLEON III.

A

LAMENTATION
ON
REPUBLICAN FRANCE.

BY

EDWARD ST. JOHN-BRENNAN.
AUTHOR OF "AMBROSIA AMORIS."

L'Empire c'est la paix.

ROME: GIUSEPPE VIA, 387, VIA DEL CORSO.
LONDON: JOHN CAMDEN HOTTEN, 74, 75, PICCADILLY.
1870.

Price Sixpence.

With the Author's Compts

A
LAMENTATION
ON
REPUBLICAN FRANCE.

Shall we have a Republic? . . . . No, gentlemen, revolution is poison. We have long enough been the dupes of delusion, the aspish breath of its heralders have fretted our spleen, and turned the honey of our lives to gall. The revolutionary banner will have been unfurled. And at this moment I see looming in the distance . . . Revolutionism standing on the precipice of that abyss which yawns for the annihilation of the State of England, and the archangel of our British Constitution shrieking out, in his might and in his power, to our hearts—*Beware ye men of England!*

From a speech, by the Author, to the Electors of the City of Gloucester. Nov. 9th. 1868.

A LAMENTATION ON REPUBLICAN FRANCE.

BY

EDWARD ST. JOHN-BRENNAN.
AUTHOR OF "AMBROSIA AMORIS."

L'Empire c'est la paix.

ROME: GIUSEPPE VIA, 387, VIA DEL CORSO.
LONDON: JOHN CAMDEN HOTTEN, 74, 75, PICCADILLY.
1870.

23474.7

College Library.
Nov. 14, 1901.
OWELL BEQUEST

DEDICATED,

With profound respect and admiration,

TO

HIS IMPERIAL MAJESTY

NAPOLEON III.

BY THE GRACE OF GOD AND THE WILL OF THE NATION,

EMPEROR OF THE FRENCH

BY

his humble and very obedient servant

EDWARD St. JOHN-BRENNAN

PALAZZO TOMATI, VIA SISTINA,
ROME.
OCTOBER. 15, 1870.

A LAMENTATION
ON
REPUBLICAN FRANCE.

I.

An emperor smitten, not slain,
  Smitten sore by the treason of knaves,
Thou shalt rise, O Napoleon, to crush
  'Neath thy heel those abortions of slaves,
'Neath thy heel shalt thou crush them to death,
Those who have poisoned with pestilent breath
The good thou hast done for thy beautiful France
In the days of thy might and magnificence.

II.

Cry aloud all ye minions of hate,
   Of envy, of power and lust!
Cry aloud in your wrath as ye may!
   For God blinds you all as with dust.
With the dust of your shame and your guilt,
   The dust of your treacherous lies;
For the dust of the land whereon blood was
     spilt
   Hath blinded your reason for sacrifice.

III.

The days of your greatness are numbered,
   Days sick with contagion and sin,
For the warrior Vengeance hath slumbered
   Awhile, till in laughter he win,
Leaving you, O ye fungi of conquest,
   To revel and rail in your power.

But lo! ye shall fall, being stricken,
 As the night's frost striketh the flower.
In the eve ye shall raise your red eyes,
 Republican, bloodshot, and dim,
Ye shall raise them to stare at the pomp
 Wherein ye would each supplant him,—
Him your lord by the grace of your God,
 Lord of France by its peoples' will.
But at dawn ye shall see all your hopes
 Like grass on a sterile hill
Sun-stricken and dead, and delivered
 To reapers, to garner and spoil,
To burn and to purge as with fire
 Fed to fierceness with blood as with oil.
Then mocked in your dark hour of trouble,
 Your hour of passionate pain,
Your bitterest cup shall pass, poisoned
 With hate and the dregs of disdain.

IV.

Republican Rule — why by heavens!
  The wrath of delusion was full
When it made ye seek the fell byeway
  That led to an impotent lull.
A lull from War's swift-spreading passion,
  A lull of confusions and fears,
That shall rend thee in pieces, O France,
  And leave but the dowry of tears.

V.

I have heard in the days of thy glory,
  Thy days of republican fame,
That thou, O fair France, with dire gory
  Red hands, called on God in thy shame,
The shame of great temples destroyed,
  The shame of revulsion and blood;
For this shame didst thou call upon God
  To dam its soul-surfeiting flood.

He stayed it, and gave thee an empire,
   And ruler whose heart pined for peace;
But you, O ye demons of terror,
   Ye fiends of destruction and war,
Made his anguish and trouble increase.
   He would hold you in hand as a rider,
But a rider that knows not his horse,
   He would rein you while ye would encompass
The world and its all, but your corse
   Shall be turned to a sigh-swolen pillow
For Victory's vanguard of power,
   And ye red-capped shall droop as a willow
That weeps in your desolate hour.
   O thou France! cast them down from their places,
Whereto they have clambered by lies;
   Cast them down ere with blood-begrimed faces

These traitors enslave you—their prize,
To ravish, to wreck and despise.
   The prize of deception and fraud
Art thou, O my Emperor's France!
   Wilt thou then be the serf of deceit?
   Nay; strangle these dogs at thy feet,
And maintain thine omnipotence!
Think you knaves that I cry with vain cry
   Calling him to thy throne, he who slew
The python of terror and blood,
   The serpent that vanquished you?
It shall be when the season hath gathered
   The fruits that are ripe with desire,
That a Bonaparte, laureled and crowned,
   Shall build peace on thy wasted pyre.

VI.

England! thy friend and thy fellow
   In peace, desolation and war,

Was Napoleon, a prince of the people,
    A splendour-absorbing star.
The sad hour of trial oft triumphs,
    And lingers to season our hopes;
Yet the moment must come when mid tempests
    The spectre of sorrow elopes
With the griefs that are burthened with pity,
    A pity that stings us like gall.
Ah! 'twere better such mean-portioned bliss
    Were not Time's for life's interval.
Thou my Albion! sea-cintured and mighty,
    For thee is my bosom made full
Of a love for the hope when thy children
    Shall crown thee as Terrible;
Not in war, not in bloodshed, but truth
    The terrible champion of right,
Shalt thou be, O island of freedom!
    O island of beauty and ruth!

For the sunshine of reason is thine,
    The sunshine that baffles the night,
The night of sedition and discord,
    Disunion and traitorous ken,
The blackness and darkness of schism,
    The slayer of honour in men.
An honour of dissolute passion,
    The kin of dishonour and fear,
The demon of desparate terror
    That wakes with the chanticleer.
Wakes pallid and husky at dawn,
    Awaiting the blush of the morn,
When tyranny rampant unfurles
    The standard of slaughter and scorn.
A banner dyed crimson with lust,
    The lust of an earthly power,
The lust of fermented hope,
    The lust of a transient hour

Of rule mock-imperial, with palace
   Decked out in the glitter of sin,
Fraternity shouted abroad,
   While enmity reigneth within.
On high writ in letters of blood
   Equality, Liberty breathes;
While the hearts of the rulers make feast
   O'er the pot where your slavery seethes.
Out on inane republican freedom!
   Man was born to serve and to rule:
Think ye, O ye sons of delusion,
   The wise man will feast with the fool?
I tell thee they mock thee to nourish
   Their hopes of ambitious despair,
They crumble thy temples of greatness
   To build themselves fortunes—Beware!
Beware, O my France, they are traitors,
   They whet thy keen anguish with words,

A LAMENTATION

Till they yield thee all-wasted with treason
   To strife and internal swords.
If honour thy dream be, O mother,
   Make recompense now for thy sin;
Give the nephew the balm of thy friendship,
   And thus thy state-penance begin.
By the side of his armies have fallen
   Our lovers, our fathers, our braves,
By their side have we conquered fair cities
   Despoiling the monarch of slaves.[1]
Stretch thine arms and aid him, lest thou
   In the moment of labour and pain
Shalt cry to the nations for help,
   But shalt cry *desolation* in vain.

---

[1] *The Crimea, forget not, ye Britons!*
   There, were sons of an empire slain;
When Nicholas tyrant of Russia
   Gorged in blood his desire of gain.

ON REPUBLICAN FRANCE.

Beware! lest the serpent ye slay not
   Spit at you the venom of death;
Beware! lest it dull thy wreath's jewel
   With the fumes of its sickening breath;
Beware! lest it smite thee in darkness,
   Smite thee sore on the joint of thy hip;
Beware! lest it trap thee in folly,
   And slay with seductive lip.
Beware! lest the mantle of crimson,
   And cap of republican red,
Clothe thee, England, in hot revolution,
   And pall the bright crown on thine head.
Beware of the furies of fate!
   Beware! for the current strong
That swept from Imperial France
   A throne pilastered with song.

VII.

Thy white-livered sons, O Napoleon,—
   God be thanked there's a holier few, —
Turned and smote thee her great benefactor;
   But them shall God smite raising you
To the throne of your glory and greatness,
   The throne of your race and your line,
Whose pillars were wisdom and light
   From on high and divine.
Bright peace-crowning days, sure, must come
   With swift wing, for true majesty reigns
In the hearts of the strong sons of men,
   In our loins and our reins.
Glory lives: but, alas! who can tell
   When the day of completion shall come?
When Truth shall reign upon earth,
   And hatred and lying be dumb?

Days as yet are but clothèd in hours
   Whose raiment is tattered and thin,
And the bones of their skeleton, Shame,
   Are damp with deception and sin.
Days still feed on slander and cunning,
   On hate and a traitor's kiss;
Yet abide but a span and war's trial
   Shall purge life of lust such as this!
Abide all ye sons of the Empire!
   Death's spreading her awful pall;
Anon mid the thunder of nations
   Thy republic, O Paris, shall fall
As a leaf sere and withered in Autumn,
   Dry, sapless, and parched at the stem;
Thou shalt fall, driven on by the tempest
   Of scorn, lisping faintly at them
Whom you smote in the days of your treason,
   The days of your passionate power,

Lisping faintly as fluttering leaf—
The poison of ruin is sour.

VIII.

Germania! thy time's in its fulness,
   Thy might is in Europe made known,
And thy glory, republican horror,
   Hath jewelled the wreathe of thy crown.
Thou art great in thy strife and thy union:
   War-trailed with the laughter of death
Thou hast broken the wings of the eagle,
   And stricken with sighings its breath.
For purged were the hearts of thy children
   From treason and traitorous spleen,
When arrogant France would dis-sever
   The concord that made thee a queen.
A queen clothed in raiment of light,
   With reason encircling thy fame,

A queen that consorted with right
    In the regal array of thy name.
Thou art great for earth's princes applaud thee,
    The kings and the rulers of states,
They applaud thee, and deck thee with honours
    Out-reaching the favouring fates.
They have given thee faith and forbearance,
    And time-serving peace in thy van;
They have given thee praise for compassion,
    Enwreathing the work you began.
Thus blazoned with pride and laudations,
    With wrathful and ravenous fire
Ye shall raze the republic of rebels,
    And sow it with salt of desire.

IX.

O God! how the months are in blossom,
    The nights and the swift-fleeing hours,

Full-flooded with weeping and anguish,
  And fraught with all-conquering powers!
It shall come to pass in thy sorrow
  That thou overtaken shalt weep,
As the furies of utter destruction
  Encompass thy death in thy sleep.
When thou slumberest secure in thy cities,
  Well bastioned with walls and with men,
Thou shalt fall being unto thine armies
  As a lamb in a lion's den.
Thou shalt fall, O republican France,
  In the days when God's vengeance is full;
Thou shalt fall, while with uplifted voice
The nations about thee rejoice
  With a joy that's unspeakable.

X.

Ye traitors stiff-hearted with discord,
  Having reaped where ye dare not sow,

ON REPUBLICAN FRANCE.

Brought unto thy France with pollution,
   Lamentation, mourning and woe.
Ye brought to thy land desolation,
   Ye gave her the potion of blood
That poisons the mightiest nations,
   That embitters the well-spring of good.
Ye turned and smote her, your mother,
   Ye lifted your voices on high,
Till drunk with the passion of conquest
   Ye lied as but traitors lie.
O'er your ways hung the pall of deception,
   Black, dismal, filthy, defiled
With the lust of the hate that you nourished
   For him whom your leasing beguiled.
But ye shall all-suppliant humble
   Yourselves to the lord of your ways;
Shall suppliant ask him for pardon,
   For brighter and bloodless days.

A LAMENTATION

But hearing you, he shall not hearken,
Till mournful sorrows shall darken
The splendour and sunshine of hope
   In the shadowless valley of death,
Where the angel of wrath stands to slay you
   With desire that glisteneth
In the light of the powers triumphant,
   And the flickering sheen of despair
That flashes from treason demented
   Fulfilling its destiny there.
Even there on thy vineyards and gardens
   Thy blood as rich red wine shall flow,
And thy scarlet berretto be trampled
   By hoof of war-horse and by sow.
Swine—swine whose gross entrails are whet
   With a feverish lust that shall turn,
Keen whet with the salt tears of blood

That course through our life's-veins and
    burn.
Swine cleanless, whose bristles are fire,
    Whose tusks rend the wounded and dead,
Whose palate is throbbing and parched
    For the blood of the vanquishèd.
Ye shall see, O ye kindred of treason,
    Ye fellows of foul-trodden ways,
The hours crowned with empire and justice,
    The work of thy turbulent days.
Ye shall see this and faint in your terror;
    For then shall the eyes that were dim
Be opened to see that the nations
    Mock you in exalting him.

XI.

O ye that are heavy of lip,
    And ye that are hollow of heart,

A LAMENTATION

Your doom with a desperate flash
   Hath caused your confusion to start
Like hell's flames, infernal and furious,
   That leck the foundations of heaven,
And sweep by its temples immortal
   In whirlwinds wrathfully driven.
Ye sorcerers, whelps of a demon,
   And suckled by serpentine teat,
Ye slaughtered the fetich that bore you,
   And drank of the brine of her feet.
But thou shalt be torn into pieces,
   Thy bowels cast unto the dogs,
And the filth of the womb of thy mother
   A festival portion for hogs.
Come out from amongst them ye loyal!
   They would rend you for spoil and for gain;
Come out! desolation's upon them;
   They are trapped in the travail of pain.

ON REPUBLICAN FRANCE.

Come out! for the furies of slaughter
    Cling close to their gory-red trail;
Come out! ere the cries of thy children
    Thy desolate ruin bewail.
Come out of them! Come! O my people!
    Oppression grows wild with despair;
Come out ere the strumpet of treason
    Make fulsome the fire-fretted air!
Come out! for the God of thy fathers
    Calls to earth for oblations of blood;
Come out! ere the demon of darkness
    Bind thy brows with a death-stricken hood.
There are years that are full of displeasure,
    Years eager for anguish and toil,
Years pent with soul-pangs of full measure,
    And years that are meted for spoil.
But then when unburthened of weepings,
    Unladen of sorrow and sin,

The heart cries aloud in its lightness,
  And new years unfettered begin.

XII.

Awake from thy stupor, O France,
  And shatter thy shackles of woe!
Awake to thy freedom and live
  As thou livedst long ago!
Let the dream of thy night and thy grief
  Fulfil all thy visions of power:
When thou wakest awake with a shout,
  And in bloom like a dew-sprinkled flower.
Let the foulness of festered deceit
  Search the heart of republican ways,
Till sick with the gangrene of lust
  They shriek for the gathering of days.
Their sorcery, wasted with leasing,
  The gluttonous slave of desire,

Sweats spent and soul-saturated,
  Sweats spent like a slow-smothered fire.
Like a furnace wherein is a serpent
  That hisses and spits in its pain,
A furnace wherein sorrow's tears
  Hiss sharply like fierce lightning-rain.
Peace sodden and supple and dead,
  Fears smitten with doubt and despair,
Gather high and envelope thy head,
  And the desolate ruin hung there.
In your glory, O France, and your greatness,
  Avenge not these sorely with death;
Yea rather supplant their affliction
  With joy that encompasseth
The years of your gladness and pleasaunce
  Years fashioned and garnered with grace,
Fashioned fair with the spoil of pollution
  Distent in thy leperous face.

A LAMENTATION

For them let destruction be severed,
   Let Treason be swept in the wind;
In the birth of their impotent fancies
   Let war and oppression be twinned.
For them be remembrance forgotten,
   Remembrance that smoulders to hate,
Remembrance, regenerate risen
   With leaven that labours with fate.
For them let that mystical symbol,
   Republicans' wanton device,
Allure them to death and to slaughter
   As vipers for sacrifice.
Cry aloud, O fair France, cry aloud
   'Gainst the bonds of republican chains!
Lest the angel of death in his wrath
   Scatter tares on your blood-sweltered plains.
Cry aloud, with a subtle-struck grief,
   For thy lover, the lord of thy life!

Cry aloud! lest thou woo him in blood,
   And regret thy divorcement in strife.
He shall press thee with joy to his bosom,
   Clasp thy lips with an arrogant kiss,
And endow thee with summer-wreathed hours,
   And nights of a somnolent peace.
O France! from the grave of thy sorrow,
   With the ardour of passionate faith,
Thou shalt rise from thy ashes of mourning
   Like a Phoenix re-strengthened by death.

XIII.

O Emperor! smitten, not slain,
   Smitten sore by the treason of knaves,
Thou shalt rise, O Napoleon, to crush
   'Neath thy heel those abortions of slaves,
'Neath thy heel shalt thou crush them to death,
Those who have poisoned with pestilent
   breath

The good thou hast done for thy beautiful
   France
In the days of thy might and magnificence.

THE END THAT IS THE BEGINNING.

Printed by Libri Plureos GmbH in Hamburg, Germany